Making the most of
FILLING & HEALTHY

WeightWatchers®

Making the most of
FILLING & HEALTHY

CAROL TENNANT

SIMON &
SCHUSTER
ILLUSTRATED

London · New York · Sydney · Toronto · New Delhi

A CBS COMPANY

The recipes

All of the recipes in this book use foods from either the Filling & Healthy food list or the Flavour Boosters list. For that reason, and to make it a bit easier for you, we have not highlighted any of these foods in green as we normally would. You may also find that some of the cook's tips use foods that are not included on either of these lists – if this is the case, and you're following the Filling & Healthy day approach, we have pointed out that you may need to use some of your weekly *ProPoints* allowance if you were to include these in the recipe.

All of the recipe ingredients have quantities listed, however, if you are following the Filling & Healthy day approach you need only use these as a guide as there is no need to weigh or measure anything.

 You'll find a *ProPoints* values index on page 96. This tells you how many *ProPoints* values per serving each recipe contains. The index is listed in *ProPoints* value order to make it easy for you to search.

If you see this symbol beside a recipe, it means that healthy oils (olive, safflower, sunflower, flaxseed or rapeseed) have been used – remember, if you're following the Filling & Healthy day approach and you have already used your 2 daily teaspoons, you'll need to count this out of your weekly allowance.

V This means the recipe is suitable for vegetarians. Where relevant, free-range eggs, vegetarian cheese, vegetarian virtually fat-free fromage frais, vegetarian low fat crème fraîche and vegetarian low fat yogurts are used. Virtually fat-free fromage frais, low fat crème fraîche and low fat yogurts may contain traces of gelatine so they are not always suitable for a vegetarian diet – just check the labels.

❄ This means you can freeze this dish. There may be specific freezing instructions so just check the recipe to be sure.

The small print

Eggs We use medium eggs, unless otherwise stated. Pregnant women, the elderly and children should avoid recipes with eggs which are not fully cooked or raw.
Low fat spread When a recipe uses a low fat spread, we mean a spread with a fat content of no less than 38%.
Microwaves If we have used a microwave in any of our recipes, the timings will be for an 850 watt microwave oven.
Prep and cooking times These are approximate and meant to be guidelines. Prep time includes all the steps up to and following the main cooking time(s).
Low fat soft cheese Where a recipe uses low fat soft cheese, we mean a soft cheese with a fat content of less than 5%.

First published in Great Britain by
Simon & Schuster UK Ltd, 2014
A CBS Company

Copyright © 2014, Weight Watchers
International, Inc.

SIMON & SCHUSTER
ILLUSTRATED BOOKS
Simon & Schuster UK Ltd
222 Gray's Inn Road
London WC1X 8HB
www.simonandschuster.co.uk
Simon & Schuster Australia, Sydney
Simon & Schuster India, New Delhi

Weight Watchers, *ProPoints* and the
ProPoints icon are the registered
trademarks of Weight Watchers
International Inc. and used under license
by Weight Watchers (UK) Ltd. All rights
reserved.

Weight Watchers Publications Team:
Imogen Prescott, Nina McKerlie
Photography: William Shaw
Food preparation: Sue Ashworth
Prop styling: Jenny Iggleden

For Simon & Schuster Illustrated
Director of Illustrated Publishing:
Ami Stewart
Senior Commissioning Editor: Nicky Hill
Art Director: Corinna Farrow
Production Manager: Katherine Thornton
Design: Miranda Harvey, Richard Proctor

Colour Reproduction by
Dot Gradations Ltd, UK
Printed and bound in Italy

A CIP catalogue record for this book
is available from the British Library

ISBN: 978-1-47113-477-7

Pictured on front cover: Slow-Cooked
Beef Meatball Stew, page 60
Pictured on back cover from left to right:
Turkey Club Sandwich, page 10; Steak and
Chunky Chips with Herbed Hollandaise,
page 86; Creamy Mushroom Rostis,
page 70
Pictured on front flap: Chicken and
Roasted Squash Salad, page 36
Pictured on back flap: Sweet Potato
and Spinach Curry, page 72

CONTENTS

INTRODUCTION

How this cookbook can work best for you...

If you're following the Filling & Healthy day approach, every recipe in this book has been written especially for you! Made up entirely of foods from the Filling & Healthy food list along with some Flavour Boosters, every recipe you make can be eaten safe in the knowledge that you won't have to count anything at all.

...No matter where you are in your journey

And don't worry if you have moved on to counting everything, this cookbook is still for you. All you need to do is turn to the handy *ProPoints* values index on page 96 where you can see exactly how many *ProPoints* values you will need to use for each recipe. This makes it really easy to follow the plan while cooking from scratch as there is no guesswork involved.

And remember...

Filling & Healthy foods are at the heart of the *ProPoints* system, helping you to fill up faster and stay fuller for longer – so get cooking and love the food you eat.

Weight Watchers and the ProPoints plan

Food is our fuel, and it's all around us every day. It's time to put yourself back in control of the food choices you make. Weight Watchers gives you a plan to help you achieve this and you can adapt it according to your personal preference – whether you want to take a simple approach or a more flexible approach, the choice is yours. Find out more at weightwatchers.co.uk

LIGHT
Meals

Turkey club sandwich 10

Mini chicken, spinach and cottage cheese frittatas 12

Hearty spiced mixed bean soup 14

Cheesy potato topper 16

Butter bean toast topper 18

Spanish eggs with potatoes and peppers 20

Home-made chip-shop chips with curry sauce 22

Spicy beans on toast 24

Chinese-style white fish 26

Crispy potato skins 28

Eggs Benedict 30

Yellow split pea and ham soup 32

TURKEY
Club Sandwich

A great way to use up leftover turkey – but equally good with
wafer thin turkey from the supermarket.

Makes 1 sandwich
Takes 10 minutes

3 slices calorie controlled brown
    bread, such as Weight Watchers
    Brown Danish
4 smoked bacon medallions
2 tablespoons quark
½ teaspoon Dijon mustard, or more,
    to taste
a squeeze of lemon juice, or more,
    to taste
75 g (2¾ oz) sliced skinless turkey
    breast
1 large tomato, sliced thinly
crisp lettuce, such as Little Gem or
    Iceberg
salt and freshly ground black pepper

1 Lightly toast the bread on both sides and grill the bacon.
Meanwhile, mix together the quark, mustard, lemon juice and a
little seasoning to taste, adding more mustard or lemon if you like.
When the bread is toasted, spread the quark mixture on 2 slices.

2 Divide the turkey between the two slices, then top with the
grilled bacon, followed by the tomato and lettuce. Season again
to taste. Stack one slice on top of the other, and top with the final
slice of bread. Cut the sandwich in half on the diagonal and put a
cocktail stick through each half to hold it together.

Cook's tips Instead of the quark mixture, add some mayonnaise
using **ProPoints** values from your weekly allowance.

If you prefer, use a brown sandwich thin in place of the three slices
of bread and put all the filling between the two slices.

MINI CHICKEN,
Spinach and Cottage Cheese Frittatas

Quick to make, these baked frittatas are really filling and
they're ideal to pop in a lunchbox.

Makes 8 frittatas
Preparation time 10 minutes
Cooking time 25 minutes

calorie controlled cooking spray
150 g (5½ oz) baby spinach
200 g (7 oz) cooked skinless chicken
    breast, torn into small chunks
3 spring onions, chopped finely
100 g (3½ oz) natural cottage cheese
6 eggs
2 tablespoons finely chopped
    fresh dill
salt and freshly ground black pepper

To serve
mixed salad
fat-free salad dressing

1 Preheat the oven to Gas Mark 5/190°C/fan oven 170°C. Spray
8 holes of a non-stick 12-hole muffin tin with cooking spray.

2 Put the spinach in a colander. Pour a kettleful of boiling water
over the leaves to wilt them. Then run cold water over the leaves to
stop them cooking. Leave to drain. When cool enough to handle,
squeeze as much excess moisture from the spinach as you can (do
this in small handfuls), then chop roughly.

3 Divide the chicken, chopped spinach, spring onions and cottage
cheese between the muffin cases. Beat the eggs with the dill and
season well. Divide the beaten eggs between the prepared muffin
tin holes. It may look like there isn't enough egg, but the mixture
will rise during cooking. Bake for 20–25 minutes until risen and
golden.

4 Allow the frittatas to cool briefly, before serving with a large
mixed salad dressed with fat-free salad dressing.

Cook's tip Reduce the cottage cheese to 50 g (1¾ oz) and
add 50 g (1¾ oz) grated reduced fat Cheddar using **ProPoints**
values from your weekly allowance, dividing it equally between
the frittatas.

HEARTY SPICED
Mixed Bean Soup

A brilliant winter warmer of a soup, full of vegetables and beans.

Serves up to 4
Takes 40 minutes

calorie controlled cooking spray
1 onion, chopped finely
1 carrot, chopped finely
1 celery stick, chopped finely
1 green chilli, de-seeded and
    chopped finely
1 garlic clove, crushed
2 teaspoons ground cumin
1 teaspoon smoked paprika
1 teaspoon dried oregano
400 g can chopped tomatoes
2 x 400 g cans mixed beans in water,
    drained and rinsed
700 ml (1¼ pints) vegetable stock,
    from a cube
2 tablespoons chopped fresh
    coriander, plus a few sprigs to
    garnish
salt and freshly ground black pepper

1 Heat a large lidded saucepan over a medium heat and spray with the cooking spray. When hot, add the onion, carrot and celery. Cook, stirring often, until softened – about 10 minutes – adding a little water if the vegetables start to stick.

2 Add the green chilli and garlic and stir briefly before adding the cumin, paprika and dried oregano. Stir once again, then add the tomatoes, beans and vegetable stock. Bring to the boil, reduce the heat to a simmer, cover and cook for 20 minutes, until all the vegetables are soft.

3 Season to taste, then stir in the coriander. Serve immediately, garnished with coriander sprigs.

Cook's tips Serve with some home-made tortilla chips made from Weight Watchers tortillas cut into wedges, sprayed with calorie controlled cooking spray and baked until crisp.

Using **ProPoints** values from your weekly allowance, sprinkle some grated reduced fat Cheddar over each portion.

CHEESY POTATO
Topper

A quick filling idea –for a plain baked potato.

(V) Makes 4 potatoes
Takes 1 hour

4 x 250 g (9 oz) baking potatoes,
    pierced several times with a fork
400 g (14 oz) natural cottage cheese
160 g (5¾ oz) 0% fat Greek yogurt
4 spring onions, chopped finely
1 tablespoon finely chopped mixed
    fresh herbs (such as chives, basil,
    dill), plus extra to serve
salt and freshly ground black pepper
cherry tomatoes and mixed leaves,
    to serve

1 Preheat the oven to Gas Mark 7/220°C/fan oven 200°C. Bake the potatoes for 20 minutes, then reduce the temperature to Gas Mark 6/200°C/fan oven 180°C for a further 30–40 minutes, or until a skewer inserted in the potatoes passes through easily.

2 Meanwhile, mix together the cottage cheese, Greek yogurt, spring onions and herbs. Season to taste.

3 When the potatoes are cooked through, remove from the oven and cut them open. Divide the cottage cheese mixture between the potatoes, sprinkle with a few more chopped herbs, and serve immediately with cherry tomatoes and salad leaves.

Cook's tip For non-vegetarians, add some crispy fried bacon medallions. You won't use up any of your weekly ***ProPoints*** allowance as they are on the Filling & Healthy food list.

BUTTER BEAN
Toast Topper

Butter beans make a creamy toast topper, perfect for a speedy but tasty lunch.

(v) Makes 4 slices
Takes 15 minutes

calorie controlled cooking spray
1 garlic clove, chopped finely
a sprig of fresh rosemary, leaves
    removed and chopped finely
2 tomatoes, peeled, de-seeded
    and chopped roughly
zest of 1 lemon
400 g can butter beans in water,
    drained and rinsed
75–100 ml (3–3½ fl oz) vegetable
    stock, from a cube
2 brown sandwich thins
salt and freshly ground black pepper
chopped red onion and chives,
    to garnish

1 Heat a medium saucepan or small non-stick frying pan over a medium heat and spray with the cooking spray. When hot, add the garlic and rosemary and stir together briefly before adding the tomatoes, lemon zest and beans. Stir in the vegetable stock, bring to the boil, and simmer for 10 minutes until the tomatoes have started to break down. Remove from the heat.

2 Using a fork, roughly mash about a third to a half of the beans, until the mixture is quite thick. Season well. Meanwhile, toast the sandwich thins.

3 Arrange the 4 slices of toasted bread on a serving plate, and divide the bean mixture between the slices. Serve immediately, sprinkled with red onion and chives.

Cook's tip Drizzle with a teaspoon of extra virgin olive oil from your 2 daily teaspoons of healthy oil or from your weekly *ProPoints* values allowance.

SPANISH EGGS
with Potatoes and Peppers

This great dish tastes of summer and makes an easy weekend lunch or brunch.

(V)

Serves up to 4
Takes 35 minutes

350 g (12 oz) new potatoes, halved
    or quartered if large
calorie controlled cooking spray
1 onion, sliced
1 red pepper, de-seeded and sliced
    thickly
2 garlic cloves, sliced
2 teaspoons smoked paprika
250 g (9 oz) whole cherry tomatoes
1 tablespoon chopped fresh flat leaf
    parsley, plus extra to serve
4 eggs
salt and freshly ground black pepper

1 Put the potatoes in a large saucepan and cover with water. Bring to the boil and simmer for 10–12 minutes until the potatoes are tender. Drain well.

2 Meanwhile, heat a large non-stick frying pan over a medium heat and spray with the cooking spray. Add the onion and pepper and cook for 5 minutes until starting to soften. Add the garlic and continue to cook for a further 5–7 minutes until starting to brown.

3 Tip in the cooked potatoes, smoked paprika and cherry tomatoes with a good splash of water, and cook until the tomatoes are starting to break up, stirring often – about another 5–7 minutes. As the tomatoes start to soften, break some of them up with the back of a wooden spoon to make a sauce. Add a little more water if necessary. Stir in the parsley and season to taste. Transfer the mixture to a serving plate and wipe clean the frying pan.

4 Return the pan to the heat, and spray with the cooking spray. Break in the eggs, one at a time. Fry to your liking. Serve the eggs with the potato and pepper mixture, sprinkled with parsley and black pepper.

Cook's tip Instead of using smoked paprika, add some chopped chorizo using **ProPoints** values from your weekly allowance. Add it with the onion and pepper.

HOME-MADE CHIP-SHOP CHIPS
with Curry Sauce

A great treat any day of the week – the curry sauce is just delicious.

(V) Serves up to 4
Takes 55 minutes

(❄) Freeze sauce only

4 x 250 g (9 oz) potatoes, such as
    Maris Piper, unpeeled
calorie controlled cooking spray
salt and freshly ground black pepper

For the curry sauce
½ onion, chopped finely
1 garlic clove, crushed
½ teaspoon finely chopped fresh root
    ginger
2 teaspoons Madras curry powder
200 g can chopped tomatoes
2 teaspoons artificial sweetener
25 g (1 oz) virtually fat-free fromage
    frais
1 tablespoon chopped fresh
    coriander
1 tablespoon chopped fresh mint

1 Preheat the oven to Gas Mark 7/220°C/fan oven 200°C. Slice the potatoes thickly, then cut the slices across into chips. Transfer the chips to a large roasting tray and spray with the cooking spray. Season well and toss the chips to coat. Transfer the tray to the preheated oven, and cook for 40–50 minutes, turning every 10–15 minutes, until the chips are golden and tender.

2 Meanwhile, make the curry sauce. Spray a large saucepan with the cooking spray, add the onion and cook over a medium heat for 5–7 minutes until soft. Add the garlic and ginger and cook for a further minute. Add the curry powder and cook for a further 1–2 minutes until it smells fragrant and the onion mixture is coated in the curry powder.

3 Add the tomatoes, 2–3 tablespoons of water and the sweetener. Stir well and bring to the boil. Reduce the heat and simmer, uncovered, for 12–15 minutes until thickened.

4 Carefully transfer the sauce to a blender or food processor and blend until smooth, or mash with a potato masher. Return to the pan and add the fromage frais, fresh herbs and seasoning. Stir well, and heat through very gently before serving – do not boil or the fromage frais will split the sauce and make it look curdled. Serve the chips with the curry sauce on the side.

Cook's tip Use sugar from your weekly **ProPoints** allowance instead of the artificial sweetener, if you prefer.

SPICY BEANS
on Toast

A great way to liven up a can of good old baked beans and make a really tasty meal.

 Serves up to 4
Takes 25 minutes

calorie controlled cooking spray
1 onion, chopped finely
1 green chilli, de-seeded and
    chopped finely
½ teaspoon ground cumin
1 teaspoon ground coriander
400 g can reduced sugar and salt
    baked beans
12 cherry tomatoes, quartered
2 tablespoons chopped fresh
    coriander
4 slices calorie controlled brown
    bread or 2 brown sandwich
    thins, split
salt and freshly ground black pepper

1 Heat a medium saucepan over a medium heat and spray with the cooking spray. Add the onion and green chilli and cook for 5–7 minutes until the onion is soft. Add the cumin and coriander and stir for a further minute. Add the can of baked beans and the cherry tomatoes and bring to the boil.

2 Reduce the heat and simmer for 10–12 minutes until the tomatoes have softened. Stir in the fresh coriander and adjust the seasoning to taste.

3 Meanwhile, toast the bread or thins on both sides and arrange on some plates. Spoon the beans over each piece of toast and serve immediately.

Cook's tip Top with a little grated Cheddar using **ProPoints** values from your weekly allowance and flash under the grill to melt it.

CHINESE-STYLE
White Fish

Poached in a flavourful broth with lots of fresh vegetables, this fish dish makes a light but filling supper.

Serves up to 4
Takes 35 minutes

300 g (10½ oz) dried brown rice
300 ml (10 fl oz) fish stock,
    from a cube
1 tablespoon soy sauce, plus extra
    to serve
2.5 cm (1 inch) fresh root ginger,
    peeled and shredded
1 garlic clove, chopped finely
4 x 150 g (5½ oz) fillets of white fish,
    such as pollock, cod, haddock,
    coley

For the stir-fry
calorie controlled cooking spray
1 carrot, cut into matchsticks
100 g (3½ oz) bean sprouts
75 g (2¾ oz) water chestnuts, drained
    and sliced into thin rounds
150 g (5½ oz) pak choi, halved or
    quartered lengthways
100 g (3½ oz) shiitake mushrooms,
    halved and stems trimmed
4 spring onions, shredded finely
chopped fresh coriander, to serve

1 Put the rice in a large lidded saucepan and cover with at least double its volume in water. Bring to the boil. Reduce the heat and simmer, covered, for 25 minutes. Remove from the heat and leave the pan covered for a further 10 minutes.

2 Meanwhile, put the fish stock, soy sauce, ginger and garlic in another lidded saucepan just big enough to hold the fish fillets in a single layer. Bring the stock mixture to the boil, then lower in the fish. Cover the pan, return to the boil, then remove it from the heat and leave to stand for 5–7 minutes, until the fish is just cooked through.

3 While the fish is cooking, spray a large wok with the cooking spray, then heat until smoking. Add the carrot, bean sprouts, water chestnuts, pak choi and shiitake mushrooms. Stir-fry for 2–3 minutes, then add a small ladleful of the fish cooking liquid. Remove the wok from the heat and add the spring onions.

4 To serve, drain the rice if necessary and divide between plates, then top with the stir-fried vegetables. Carefully remove the fish from the poaching liquid, placing the fillets on to the plates. Ladle over a little of the poaching liquid, then sprinkle with coriander. Serve immediately, with a little extra soy sauce if you like.

Cook's tip Add a teaspoon of sesame oil to the fish poaching liquid using your 2 daily teaspoons of healthy oil or from your weekly **ProPoints** values allowance.

CRISPY
Potato Skins

Stuffed with a delicious tuna filling, these potato skins are perfect for a light lunch with a green salad on the side.

Makes 8 skins
Preparation time 15 minutes
Cooking time 1 hour 20 minutes

4 x 250 g (9 oz) potatoes, such as
    Maris Piper or King Edward
calorie controlled cooking spray
400 g can mixed bean medley (or
    mixed bean salad in water),
    drained and rinsed
200 g can tuna steak in spring water
    or brine, drained
1 small red pepper, de-seeded and
    chopped finely
1 small red onion, chopped finely
1 celery stick, chopped finely
8 cherry tomatoes, halved
1 tablespoon chopped fresh chives

For the dressing
3 tablespoons fat-free salad dressing
juice of ½ lemon
2 tablespoons virtually fat-free
    fromage frais
salt and freshly ground black pepper

1 Preheat the oven to Gas Mark 6/200°C/fan oven 180°C. Pierce the potatoes in several places and bake for approximately 1 hour, until a skewer or knife passes easily through the flesh. Remove from the oven.

2 Halve the potatoes lengthways and use a spoon to scoop out the flesh, leaving a 1 cm (½ inch) border all round the skin. Reserve the flesh.

3 Increase the oven temperature to Gas Mark 7/220°C/fan oven 200°C. Transfer the potato skins to a baking tray and spray with the cooking spray. Return to the oven for a further 15–20 minutes, until the skins are browned and crispy.

4 Meanwhile, mix together the beans, tuna, pepper, onion, celery, tomatoes and chives. Chop the reserved potato flesh roughly and add to the mixture. Make the dressing by mixing together the salad dressing, lemon juice and fromage frais. Season to taste and add to the tuna and bean mixture. Mix well.

5 When the potato skins are cooked, transfer them to a serving dish and spoon over the tuna and bean mixture. Serve immediately.

Cook's tip Add some grated reduced fat Cheddar using **ProPoints** values from your weekly allowance. Sprinkle it over the tuna topping and return the skins to the oven for a few minutes to melt the cheese.

EGGS *Benedict*

Great for Sunday brunch or any time you want a light supper.

Serves up to 4
Takes 30 minutes

8 bacon medallions
4 brown sandwich thins
1 tablespoon wine vinegar
8 eggs
salt and freshly ground black pepper
2 tablespoons finely chopped
   fresh chives, to garnish

For the hollandaise
2 eggs
1–2 teaspoons Dijon mustard
juice of 1 lemon
6 tablespoons hot water

1 Preheat the grill to high.

2 Put all the hollandaise ingredients in a small heatproof bowl. Set the bowl over a pan of simmering water so that the bowl doesn't touch the water. Whisk constantly until the sauce thickens and becomes light and foamy – about 5–6 minutes. Season to taste. Remove the pan from the heat and set aside, keeping the sauce warm and whisking occasionally while you prepare the remaining ingredients.

3 Lay the bacon medallions on a baking tray and grill until crisp and browned. Set aside and keep warm.

4 Split the sandwich thins. Toast under the grill on both sides. Set aside and keep warm.

5 Bring a large frying pan or saucepan of water to the boil and add the vinegar. Reduce the heat so the water is barely simmering and add the eggs, 4 at a time (or fewer if you find it easier). Once they are cooked to your liking – simmer for around 3–4 minutes for soft-centred eggs – remove the cooked eggs to a large bowl of warm water. Repeat with the remaining eggs.

6 To serve, top each piece of toast with a bacon medallion. Top each medallion with an egg and spoon over a little of the hollandaise. Sprinkle with chives and serve immediately.

YELLOW SPLIT PEA
and Ham Soup

This is a really hearty soup – perfect for when you need warming up.

Serves up to 4
Preparation time 10 minutes
Cooking time 1½ hours

500 g (1 lb 2 oz) yellow split peas
1 large onion, chopped finely
1 carrot, chopped finely
1 celery stick, chopped finely
200 g (7 oz) cooked smoked ham,
    torn into chunky strips
700 ml (1¼ pints) chicken stock,
    from a cube
2 bay leaves
salt and freshly ground black pepper
chopped fresh parsley, to garnish

1 Put the split peas in a colander and rinse with cold water, until the water runs clear. Drain well.

2 Put the onion, carrot and celery in a large lidded saucepan. Add the drained split peas, ham, stock, 700 ml (1¼ pints) of water and the bay leaves. Bring to the boil, removing any scum that rises with a large spoon.

3 Reduce the heat to a simmer, cover and cook very gently for 1–1½ hours, adding extra water or stock if the mixture is too thick or dry, until the split peas have softened and broken down and the vegetables are all tender. You can leave the soup as it is, slightly chunky, or purée until smooth in a blender, removing the bay leaves first, and adding a little more stock or water to adjust the texture if necessary. Season to taste and serve, sprinkled with black pepper and garnished with parsley.

Cook's tip Reheat any leftovers the next day – they'll taste just as good, though you may have to add a little more stock or water to loosen the texture.

HEARTY
Main Meals

Chicken and roasted squash salad 36

All-in-one roast chicken with garlic sauce 38

Chicken stew and rice 40

Blackened fish with fiery mango salsa 42

Sea bass with fennel, potatoes and lemon 44

Roasted salmon fillet with bacon, peas, potatoes and mint 46

Jerk fish with rice and peas 48

Pork and apple hotpot 50

Quick chilli con carne 52

Souvlaki pork with kisir 54

Classic burger with a twist 56

Braising steaks with onions and mushrooms 58

Slow-cooked beef meatball stew 60

Warm spiced quinoa salad 62

Puy lentils with roasted vegetables and cumin 64

CHICKEN
and Roasted Squash Salad

This salad tastes really good served while it's still warm – but the chilled leftovers taste just as good the next day.

Serves up to 4
Preparation time 15 minutes
Cooking time 40 minutes

2 x 165 g (5¾ oz) skinless, boneless chicken breasts
1 small butternut squash, peeled, halved lengthways and seeds removed
calorie controlled cooking spray
1 tablespoon coriander seeds
½ teaspoon chilli flakes
a large pinch of cumin seeds
2 teaspoons dried oregano
400 g can chick peas, drained and rinsed
1 slice calorie controlled brown bread, cut or torn into croûton-sized pieces
2 good handfuls of rocket leaves
1 soft round lettuce, separated into leaves
75 g (2¾ oz) sugar snap peas, sliced lengthways into shreds
salt and freshly ground black pepper

For the dressing
juice of ½ lemon
1 garlic clove, crushed
4 tablespoons low fat natural yogurt
4 teaspoons extra virgin olive oil

1 Preheat the oven to Gas Mark 6/200°C/fan oven 180°C. Season the chicken breasts and wrap in foil.

2 Cut the butternut squash into chunks or wedges, put them in a roasting tray and spray with the cooking spray. Put the tray in the oven, along with the chicken parcel, and cook for 20 minutes.

3 Meanwhile, crush the coriander seeds, chilli flakes and cumin seeds in a pestle and mortar, then stir in the oregano.

4 Remove the chicken and check that it's cooked through. If there's any trace of pink, return it to the oven for a further 5–10 minutes. Remove the cooked chicken and set aside.

5 Sprinkle the spice mixture over the squash, stir well and continue cooking for a total of 40 minutes, until soft and slightly caramelised, adding the chick peas to the roasting tin for the final 10 minutes. Set the cooked squash aside until slightly cooled.

6 Put the torn or chopped bread on a baking tray and spray with cooking spray. Bake for about 5 minutes until golden and crisp.

7 Make the dressing by whisking together the lemon juice, garlic, yogurt and olive oil until well blended.

8 To assemble the salad, mix together the salad leaves and sugar snap peas on a large platter. Tear the chicken into chunks and add to the platter, along with the squash and chick peas. Scatter with the croûtons and drizzle with the dressing.

Cook's tip Add some toasted pumpkin seeds to the salad, using **ProPoints** values from your weekly allowance.

ALL-IN-ONE ROAST CHICKEN
with Garlic Sauce

Everything cooks in one dish, saving time – and washing-up.

Serves up to 4
Preparation time 10 minutes
Cooking time 50 minutes

4 x 125 g (4½ oz) skinless chicken
    legs, visible fat removed
4 x 175 g (6 oz) potatoes, cut into
    large chunks
2 red onions, each cut into 6 wedges
8 garlic cloves, unpeeled
4 carrots, cut into large chunks
1 orange, zested, and the flesh cut
    into 8 chunks
a generous pinch of dried chilli flakes
a sprig of rosemary
2 fresh bay leaves
1 teaspoon dried thyme
calorie controlled cooking spray
250 g (9 oz) 0% fat Greek yogurt
1 tablespoon chopped fresh parsley
salt and freshly ground black pepper

1 Preheat the oven to Gas Mark 7/220°C/fan oven 200°C. Put the chicken, vegetables and orange chunks in a large roasting tin, big enough to fit everything in a single layer. Add the chilli flakes and rosemary sprig, and tuck the bay leaves in under the chicken and vegetables. Sprinkle with the dried thyme and pour in 200 ml (7 fl oz) of water. Spray everything with the cooking spray and season well.

2 Roast for 10 minutes, then turn down the oven to Gas Mark 6/200°C/fan oven 180°C. Cook for a further 30–40 minutes, until the chicken and vegetables are tender and starting to turn golden.

3 Remove from the oven and transfer the chicken and vegetables to a serving platter, discarding the bay leaves and rosemary and setting aside the garlic cloves.

4 To make the garlic sauce, squeeze the flesh from the cloves into a bowl and mash thoroughly. Stir in the yogurt, orange zest and parsley. Season to taste and serve with the chicken and roasted vegetables.

CHICKEN STEW
and Rice

Nothing beats a chicken stew on a cold night. This one is full of hearty flavours from the smoked paprika and beans.

❄

Serves up to 4
Takes 1¼ hours

calorie controlled cooking spray
8 skinless chicken drumsticks
1 large onion, chopped
2 garlic cloves, chopped finely
2 teaspoons smoked paprika
400 g can cannellini beans, drained
 and rinsed
400 g can cherry tomatoes in juice
300 g (10½ oz) dried brown rice
100 g (3½ oz) baby spinach
1 tablespoon chopped fresh parsley
salt and freshly ground black pepper

1 Spray a large lidded saucepan or flameproof casserole with the cooking spray. Add the drumsticks, in batches if necessary, and cook over a high heat, turning, until browned all over. Repeat as necessary until all the chicken is browned, removing the drumsticks to a plate.

2 Reduce the heat to medium, add the onion to the pan and cook for 5–7 minutes until softened and starting to brown. Add the garlic and stir briefly. Add the smoked paprika and stir for a further minute.

3 Add the beans and tomatoes and stir well to mix. Half fill the tomato can with water and add this to the pan, stirring well. Return the chicken to the pan and bring to the boil. Reduce the heat, cover and simmer for 30 minutes. Remove the lid and continue to simmer for a further 20–30 minutes until the chicken is tender and pulls easily from the bone.

4 Meanwhile, put the rice in a large lidded saucepan and cover with at least double its volume in water. Bring to the boil, cover and simmer very gently for 35 minutes or until tender. Drain if necessary.

5 Add the spinach to the chicken stew and stir through until wilted. Add the parsley and season to taste. Serve with the rice.

BLACKENED FISH
with Fiery Mango Salsa

Use any white fish for this dish — the skin is essential
for getting a crispy, blackened finish.

Serves up to 4
Takes 25 minutes

4 teaspoons Cajun spice mix
2 garlic cloves, crushed
1 teaspoon dried oregano
zest and juice of 2 limes
4 x 150 g (5½ oz) fillets of white fish
    (cod, pollock, haddock, coley) or
    salmon, skin on
calorie controlled cooking spray

For the mango salsa
1 large mango, peeled and cubed
    finely
½ red onion, chopped finely
1 green chilli, de-seeded and
    chopped finely
2 tablespoons chopped fresh
    coriander
zest and juice of 1 lime
salt and freshly ground black pepper

To serve
salad leaves, such as Little Gem
lime wedges

1 Make the mango salsa. Mix all the ingredients together, season to taste and set aside for the flavours to develop.

2 Mix the Cajun spice mix, garlic, oregano and lime zest and juice into a paste. Lightly score the skin of the fish, then rub the paste all over until evenly coated.

3 Heat a large non-stick frying pan until hot. Spray with the cooking spray and add the fish, skin side down. Cook for 2–3 minutes until the skin is blackened, then turn and cook for a further 1–2 minutes on the other side until just cooked. Remove from the pan and allow to rest.

4 Serve the fish with the salad leaves and salsa, plus extra lime wedges to squeeze over.

SEA BASS
with Fennel, Potatoes and Lemon

Cooking the fennel slowly ensures that it's sweet and tender.

Serves up to 4
Preparation time 10 minutes
Cooking time 1 hour

500 g (1lb 2 oz) new potatoes,
    halved if large
calorie controlled cooking spray
1 large fennel bulb, sliced thinly with
    the root removed
1 onion, sliced
1 garlic clove, sliced thinly
1 teaspoon fennel seeds, crushed
    lightly
200 ml (7 fl oz) fish or vegetable
    stock, from a cube
2 whole sea bass, approx. 800 g
    (1 lb 11 oz) each, cleaned
1 lemon, zest reserved for garnish,
    then sliced
2 sprigs of fresh thyme
2 sprigs of fresh rosemary
salt and freshly ground black pepper
2 tablespoons chopped fresh flat
    leaf parsley, to garnish

1 Preheat the oven to Gas Mark 6/200°C/fan oven 180°C. Boil the potatoes for 10–12 minutes until tender. Drain well and refresh under cold running water. Set aside.

2 Set a large frying pan over a medium heat and spray with the cooking spray. Add the fennel and onion. Reduce the heat and cook for 12–15 minutes until the fennel and onion are softened, adding a little water if necessary to stop the vegetables sticking or over browning. Add the garlic and fennel seeds and cook briefly.

3 Transfer the fennel mixture to a large ovenproof dish or roasting tin – it needs to be big enough to fit both fish side by side. Add the cooked potatoes and the fish or vegetable stock.

4 Pat the fish dry and season well. Divide the lemon slices, thyme and rosemary between the fish cavities, then lay the fish over the fennel mixture. Cover the dish with foil and transfer to the oven. Cook for 20–30 minutes until the fish is cooked through. Test it by pushing the handle of a spoon or fork into the thickest part – it should go through easily.

5 Remove from the oven, garnish with the lemon zest and parsley and serve directly from the dish.

ROASTED SALMON FILLET
with Bacon, Peas, Potatoes and Mint

Everything cooks in one roasting tin for this fabulous summer lunch or supper. Any leftovers are equally good served cold the next day.

Serves up to 4
Preparation time 10 minutes
Cooking time 45 minutes

500 g (1 lb 2 oz) new potatoes, halved if large
calorie controlled cooking spray
6 bacon medallions, cut into strips
700 g (1 lb 9 oz) whole skinless salmon fillet
200 g (7 oz) frozen peas, defrosted
4 spring onions, sliced finely
1–2 teaspoons white wine vinegar
2 tablespoons roughly chopped fresh mint
salt and freshly ground black pepper

To serve
crisp lettuce leaves
lemon wedges

1 Preheat the oven to Gas Mark 6/200°C/fan oven 180°C. Put the potatoes in a large roasting tin, spray with the cooking spray and season. Roast for 15 minutes. Scatter the bacon over the potatoes, spray with more cooking spray, and cook for a further 10 minutes until the bacon is crisp.

2 Take the tin out of the oven, push the potatoes and bacon to the sides and lay the salmon in the gap. Spray with cooking spray and season. Return the roasting tin to the oven and cook for a further 10–15 minutes, until the salmon is just cooked through.

3 Meanwhile, cook the peas for 2 minutes in boiling water, then drain well.

4 Add the peas and spring onions along with a splash of vinegar to the pan. Sprinkle with the chopped mint and serve immediately with crisp lettuce leaves and lemon wedges.

JERK FISH
with Rice and Peas

Ready-made jerk mixes and pastes are full of salt, sugar or oil.
This simplified mixture is a healthy alternative.

Serves up to 4
Preparation time 20 minutes
Cooking time 30 minutes +
    10 minutes standing

4 x 150 g (5½ oz) fish fillets, such as
    cod, pollock, hake, salmon
calorie controlled cooking spray
1 onion, chopped finely
1 carrot, chopped finely
1 celery stick, chopped finely
2 garlic cloves, chopped finely
1 teaspoon ground allspice
2 bushy sprigs of fresh thyme
200 g (7 oz) dried brown basmati rice
400 g can kidney beans, drained and
    rinsed
2 limes, halved
4 spring onions, chopped finely
salt and freshly ground black pepper

For the jerk seasoning paste
1 teaspoon mixed spice
1 tablespoon chopped fresh thyme
1 tablespoon chopped fresh
    coriander
1 or 2 hot red chillies (to taste),
    de-seeded if you prefer, roughly
    chopped
1 teaspoon grated fresh root ginger
zest and juice of 1 lime
2 spring onions, chopped roughly
½ teaspoon freshly ground black
    pepper

1 Preheat the oven to Gas Mark 6/200°C/fan oven 180°C. To make the jerk seasoning paste, put all the ingredients in the bowl of a food processor. Blend until everything is finely chopped, adding a little water if necessary to make a smooth-ish paste.

2 Rub the paste into the fish fillets and set aside while you cook the rice.

3 Spray a large, tightly lidded saucepan with the cooking spray. Put it over a medium heat and add the onion, carrot and celery and cook for 5–7 minutes until softened. Add the garlic and stir briefly, before adding the allspice, thyme and rice. Stir so that everything is well mixed, then add 600 ml (20 fl oz) water and bring to the boil. Cover the pan, reduce the heat to its lowest setting, and cook for 20 minutes. Add the beans and stir the mixture, then cover and leave to stand off the heat for 10 minutes.

4 Meanwhile, transfer the fish and halved limes to a non-stick baking tray and spray with cooking spray. Bake for 15–20 minutes or until the fish flakes easily.

5 Stir the spring onions into the rice then serve topped with the fish and a roasted lime half to squeeze over.

Cook's tip Add 1 tablespoon desiccated coconut to the rice using *ProPoints* values from your weekly allowance. Add in step 3, along with the thyme.

PORK AND APPLE
Hotpot

A twist on a classic, this hearty casserole takes almost no effort.

Serves up to 4
Preparation time 20 minutes
Cooking time 2 hours

calorie controlled cooking spray
2 onions, sliced thickly
800 g (1 lb 11 oz) boneless pork
    shoulder, trimmed of visible
    fat and cut into chunks
2 large carrots, sliced thinly
2 bushy sprigs of fresh thyme or
    1 teaspoon dried thyme
2 Granny Smith apples, cored and
    sliced thickly
900 g (2 lb) firm potatoes, such as
    Désirée, peeled and sliced thickly
700 ml (1¼ pints) hot pork or chicken
    stock, from a cube
salt and freshly ground black pepper

1 Preheat the oven to Gas Mark 3/160°C/fan oven 140°C. Heat a large non-stick frying pan over a medium heat and spray with the cooking spray. Add the onions and cook for 10–12 minutes, stirring often, until softened and lightly browned. Add a little water if necessary to stop them over-browning or sticking. Set aside.

2 In a large, lidded ovenproof casserole, layer the ingredients as follows, seasoning each layer as you go: half the onions, then half the pork, half the carrots, half the thyme, half the apples, then half the potatoes. Repeat, ending with a neat layer of potatoes. Pour in the stock.

3 Cover the casserole, transfer to the middle of the oven and cook for 1½ hours. Increase the oven temperature to Gas Mark 6/200°C/fan oven 180°C. Remove the lid and cook for a further 30 minutes or until the potatoes are browned and crispy.

Cook's tip Serve with steamed green vegetables, such as Savoy cabbage, purple sprouting broccoli and green beans.

QUICK
Chilli con Carne

A traditional chilli con carne needs to simmer for hours – this version is ready in a fraction of the time because it uses quick-cooking steak mince.

❄ Serves up to 4
Preparation time 10 minutes
Cooking time 45 minutes

calorie controlled cooking spray
500 g (1 lb 2 oz) extra lean beef
    steak mince
1 onion, chopped finely
1 carrot, chopped finely
1 celery stick, chopped finely
1 tablespoon chilli powder
1 teaspoon ground cumin
1 teaspoon dried oregano
400 g can reduced sugar and salt
    baked beans
400 g can chopped tomatoes or
    cherry tomatoes
2 tablespoons chopped fresh
    coriander
salt and freshly ground black pepper

To serve
240 g (8½ oz) dried brown rice,
    cooked according to the packet
    instructions, or 4 x 250 g (9 oz)
    baked potatoes

1 Heat a large lidded saucepan over a high heat and spray with the cooking spray. Add the steak mince and use a wooden spoon to break up the mince as it cooks. Cook for around 10 minutes, until the meat is browned. Drain off any excess fat.

2 Add the vegetables to the pan and cook for a further 5 minutes until softened. Add the chilli powder, cumin and oregano to the pan and stir briefly before adding the baked beans, tomatoes and 100 ml (3½ fl oz) water.

3 Bring to the boil, cover and simmer for 30 minutes. Remove from the heat, season to taste and stir in the coriander. Serve immediately with cooked brown rice or baked potatoes.

Cook's tip Serve with some grated reduced fat Cheddar using *ProPoints* values from your weekly allowance.

SOUVLAKI PORK
with Kisir

Kisir is the Turkish version of a bulgur wheat salad – the wheat is soaked rather than boiled, giving it a firmer, nuttier texture.

Serves up to 4

Takes 30 minutes + up to 4 hours marinating + cooling

Freeze pork only

800 g (1 lb 11 oz) lean leg of pork, visible fat removed

2 teaspoons dried mint

2 teaspoons dried oregano

juice of 1 lemon

2 garlic cloves, crushed

1 tablespoon red wine vinegar

salt and freshly ground black pepper

For the kisir

4 teaspoons olive oil

1 onion, chopped finely

1 tablespoon tomato purée

2 tomatoes, peeled and chopped

150 ml (5 fl oz) chicken or vegetable stock, from a cube

200 g (7 oz) bulgur wheat

juice of ½ lemon

1 green chilli, de-seeded and chopped finely

2 spring onions, sliced finely

2 garlic cloves, crushed

½ teaspoon ground cumin

seeds from ½ pomegranate

2 tablespoons roughly chopped fresh mint leaves

3 tablespoons roughly chopped fresh flat leaf parsley

1 Cut the pork into 2.5 cm (1 inch) chunks and put in a non-reactive bowl with the dried herbs, lemon juice, garlic and vinegar. Season, mix together well and leave to marinate for at least 30 minutes, or up to 4 hours.

2 Meanwhile, make the kisir. Heat the oil in a large saucepan over a medium heat. Add the onion and cook for 5–7 minutes until softened. Add the tomato purée and cook for a further 2 minutes, stirring constantly. Add the tomatoes and stock and bring to the boil. Remove from the heat and stir in the bulgur wheat. Add the remaining ingredients except the pomegranate seeds, mint and parsley, and leave at room temperature until cold. Season to taste.

3 Preheat the grill or a ridged grill pan. Thread the pork on to 4 skewers and cook for 6–8 minutes on each side, until golden and cooked through.

4 To serve, spread the kisir on a platter and sprinkle with the pomegranate seeds, mint and parsley. Top with the pork skewers and serve immediately.

Cook's tips Serve with some 0% fat Greek yogurt mixed with grated cucumber, garlic and mint.

When using wooden skewers, soak them first in cold water for 30 minutes or so, to prevent them from burning during cooking.

CLASSIC BURGER
with a Twist

Try this home-made burger instead of a take-away – it has all the flavour of a classic, but with a little something extra.

Makes 8 burgers
Takes 20 minutes

❄ Freeze burger only

500 g (1 lb 2 oz) extra lean
    beef mince
1 onion, grated finely
1 teaspoon dried thyme
1 teaspoon dried oregano
1 tablespoon Worcestershire sauce
salt and freshly ground black pepper

For the mustard sauce
2 tablespoons grainy mustard
5 tablespoons quark
½ Granny Smith apple, grated finely
1½–2 teaspoons Worcestershire
    sauce

To serve
brown sandwich thins or calorie
    controlled brown bread rolls,
    toasted
shredded Little Gem lettuce
sliced tomatoes

1 In a large bowl, mix together the beef mince, onion, dried herbs and Worcestershire sauce. Season well. Shape the mixture into 8 patties.

2 For the mustard sauce, mix together the mustard, quark, grated apple and Worcestershire sauce. Season well.

3 Preheat the grill or a ridged grill pan. Cook the burgers for 4–5 minutes on each side until golden and cooked through. Serve immediately on toasted sandwich thins or rolls, with the mustard sauce, lettuce and tomatoes.

Cook's tip Turn your burger into a cheese burger – add a thin slice of reduced fat Cheddar using **ProPoints** values from your weekly allowance.

BRAISING STEAKS
with Onions and Mushrooms

A wonderful warming winter dish of braised steaks in a rich sauce.

Serves up to 4
Preparation time 5 minutes
Cooking time 1½–2 hours

calorie controlled cooking spray
4 x 200 g (7 oz) lean braising steaks,
    visible fat removed
2 large onions, sliced thickly
2 garlic cloves, sliced
200 g (7 oz) button mushrooms
700 ml (1¼ pints) beef stock,
    from a cube
2 bay leaves
1 bushy sprig of fresh thyme
1 tablespoon Worcestershire sauce
salt and freshly ground black pepper

To serve
4 x 250 g (9 oz) baked potatoes or
    240 g (8½ oz) dried wholewheat
    tagliatelle, cooked according to
    the packet instructions
steamed green vegetables or salad

1 Preheat the oven to Gas Mark 4/180°C/fan oven 160°C. Spray a flameproof lidded casserole with the cooking spray and set over a medium-high heat. Add the steaks and brown well on both sides. Remove to a plate and set aside.

2 Add the onions and garlic to the casserole and cook for 5–7 minutes until softened and starting to brown. Add the mushrooms and cook for 3–4 minutes to brown slightly. Add the beef stock and stir well to pick up any brown bits in the pan. Return the steaks to the pan, along with the bay leaves, thyme and Worcestershire sauce. Bring to the boil, cover and transfer to the centre of the oven. Cook for 1½–2 hours until the meat is tender.

3 If necessary, reduce the sauce to thicken it. Remove the steaks to a plate and cover to keep warm. Put the casserole over a high heat and boil the sauce hard until thickened and reduced. Season to taste and spoon the sauce over the steaks.

4 Serve with baked potatoes or wholemeal tagliatelle and steamed green vegetables or salad.

Cook's tip Swirl a knob of butter from your weekly **ProPoints** allowance into the sauce just before serving.

SLOW-COOKED
Beef Meatball Stew

Tasty meatballs simmered in a rich tomato sauce are ideal for
a weekend supper or family lunch.

❄ Serves up to 4
Preparation time 20 minutes
Cooking time 1 hour

For the meatballs
500 g (1 lb 2 oz) extra lean
  beef mince
50 g (1¾ oz) breadcrumbs, made
  from calorie controlled brown
  bread
½ onion, grated
1 small carrot, grated
1 small courgette, grated
2 garlic cloves, crushed
1 tablespoon soy sauce
½ teaspoon each dried oregano
  and dried thyme
1 egg, lightly beaten
salt and freshly ground black pepper

For the tomato sauce
calorie controlled cooking spray
1 onion, chopped finely
1 garlic clove, crushed
1 tablespoon chopped fresh basil,
  plus extra to garnish
2 x 400 g cans chopped tomatoes
2 tablespoons tomato purée

To serve
240 g (8½ oz) dried wholewheat
  spaghetti or pasta shapes,
  cooked according to the packet
  instructions

1 Put all the ingredients for the meatballs in a large bowl. Season well and, using your hands, mix everything together thoroughly. Shape the mixture into 20 balls about the size of a walnut. Put them on a plate as you make them, and set aside while you prepare the sauce.

2 Spray a medium lidded saucepan with the cooking spray. Add the onion and cook for 5–7 minutes over a medium heat until softened. Stir in the garlic before adding the basil, tomatoes and tomato purée. Simmer the sauce while you brown the meatballs.

3 Spray a non-stick frying pan with the cooking spray and heat over a medium-high heat. Add the meatballs in batches and cook until browned, turning often. As they brown, add them to the tomato sauce. Once all the meatballs are in the sauce, bring it to the boil, cover and simmer for 1 hour until the meatballs are tender and the sauce is thick. Season to taste. Serve with wholemeal spaghetti or wholemeal pasta shapes, garnished with more fresh basil.

Cook's tips Add some grated Parmesan using **ProPoints** values from your weekly allowance.

You could also try making these meatballs with turkey breast mince, or half extra lean beef mince and half extra lean pork mince.

WARM SPICED
Quinoa Salad

Steaming quinoa gives it its fluffy texture – perfect for a salad.
Quinoa is readily available from major supermarkets.

Serves up to 4
Takes 25 minutes

V

200 g (7 oz) quinoa

400 g can black beans, drained
   and rinsed

198 g can sweetcorn, drained

1 small green pepper, chopped finely

1 small red pepper, chopped finely

1 pickled jalapeño chilli, de-seeded
   and chopped

3 spring onions, chopped finely

3 tablespoons chopped fresh
   coriander, plus a few sprigs to
   garnish

4 eggs

a pinch of paprika, to garnish

For the dressing

juice of 2 limes

a large pinch of ground cumin

4 teaspoons extra virgin olive or
   rapeseed oil

1 Wash the quinoa 4 or 5 times in a large bowl of water until the water runs relatively clear. Drain well.

2 Bring a large lidded saucepan of water to the boil, add the quinoa and simmer for 10 minutes. Drain well in a sieve. Set the sieve over a pan of simmering water, cover the quinoa with a clean tea towel and the saucepan lid. Steam for 10 minutes until fluffy and dry.

3 While the quinoa is cooking, mix together the beans, sweetcorn, peppers, jalapeño and spring onions. Whisk the dressing ingredients together and add to the bean mixture. Mix well to combine.

4 Transfer the cooked quinoa to a serving bowl and add the bean mixture along with the chopped coriander and mix well.

5 Meanwhile, poach or fry the eggs until done to your liking. Serve with the warm quinoa salad, sprinkled with paprika and garnished with coriander sprigs.

Cook's tip Use fat-free salad dressing spiked with lime and cumin for a quick alternative dressing.

PUY LENTILS
with Roasted Vegetables and Cumin

This hearty lentil dish makes a superb side to accompany grilled skinless chicken or fish.

(V) Serves up to 4
Preparation time 15 minutes
Cooking time 50 minutes

2 red onions, each cut into 6 wedges
1 red pepper, de-seeded and cut into chunks
2 carrots, cut into chunks
1 large courgette, halved lengthways and cut into chunks
8 garlic cloves, unpeeled
1½ teaspoons cumin seeds
2–3 sprigs of fresh thyme
calorie controlled cooking spray
250 g (9 oz) dried Puy lentils

For the dressing
200 g (7 oz) low fat natural yogurt
zest and juice of 1 lemon
1 tablespoon chopped fresh basil
1 tablespoon chopped fresh coriander
salt and freshly ground black pepper

1 Preheat the oven to Gas Mark 6/200°C/fan oven 180°C. Put all the vegetables, garlic, cumin seeds and thyme sprigs on a shallow roasting tray. Spray with the cooking spray and toss everything together to coat. Transfer to the oven and cook for 30 minutes.

2 Remove the tray from the oven and stir everything together, then return to the oven for a further 20 minutes until all the vegetables are tender and golden.

3 Meanwhile, put the Puy lentils in a large bowl and rinse well with at least 3 changes of water. Drain the lentils and put them in a large lidded saucepan and cover with at least double their volume of cold water. Bring to the boil, cover and simmer for about 15–20 minutes until tender. Drain well.

4 For the dressing, mix together the yogurt, lemon zest and juice, and herbs. Season to taste.

5 When the vegetables are cooked, stir in the Puy lentils. Discard the thyme sprigs before serving with the lemon and yogurt dressing.

Cook's tips Add some feta or goat's cheese using **ProPoints** values from your weekly allowance.

For extra colour, roast 200 g (7 oz) cherry tomatoes on the vine with the other vegetables, adding them for the final 10–15 minutes of cooking.

You could use 2 x 400 g cans Puy lentils in water, instead of dried.

SPEEDY
Suppers

Pan-fried chicken and asparagus 68

Creamy chicken and mushroom rostis 70

Sweet potato and spinach curry 72

Spaghetti carbonara 74

Moroccan tuna steak with a roasted pepper salsa 76

Prawn, mushroom and chick pea curry 78

Warm beetroot and smoked trout salad 80

Gammon steak with peaches and roast potato chunks 82

Steak and mushroom stroganoff 84

Steak and chunky chips with herbed hollandaise 86

Greek pork patties with radish tzatziki 88

Bacon and white bean casserole 90

Pork escalopes with caponata salad 92

PAN-FRIED CHICKEN
and Asparagus

A brilliantly quick midweek supper that's full of flavour and quite simple.

Serves up to 4
Takes 30 minutes

calorie controlled cooking spray
4 x 165 g (5¾ oz) skinless, boneless
   chicken breasts
4 smoked bacon medallions, cut into
   strips
250 g (9 oz) asparagus, trimmed
250 g (9 oz) cherry tomatoes, halved
8 large basil leaves, plus extra to
   garnish
2 tablespoons balsamic vinegar
salt and freshly ground black pepper

To serve
240 g (8½ oz) dried wholewheat
   penne, cooked according to the
   packet instructions

1 Spray a large non-stick frying pan with the cooking spray and heat over a medium-high heat. Add the chicken breasts and cook for 2–3 minutes per side. Add the bacon and asparagus. Cook for 8–10 minutes, turning the chicken, asparagus and bacon until golden and crispy. Spoon the bacon and asparagus on top of the chicken if they finish cooking before the chicken turns golden.

2 Remove the chicken, bacon and asparagus from the pan and keep warm. Add the tomatoes and basil leaves to the pan and increase the heat to high. Add a splash of water to help cook the tomatoes. Stir and simmer for a few minutes until the tomatoes have softened. Add the balsamic vinegar and bring to the boil, then season to taste.

3 Serve the chicken topped with the asparagus, bacon, tomatoes, and extra basil leaves, with some wholewheat penne pasta.

Cook's tip Add some grated Parmesan using **ProPoints** values from your weekly allowance.

CREAMY CHICKEN
and Mushroom Rostis

These substantial rostis are so tasty. You could leave out the chicken for a vegetarian version that's equally delicious.

Serves up to 4
Takes 30 minutes

2 x 165 g (5¾ oz) skinless, boneless chicken breasts, sliced thinly
200 g (7 oz) chestnut mushrooms, quartered
12 cherry tomatoes, halved
400 g (14 oz) quark
1 tablespoon chopped fresh dill, plus extra to garnish
1 tablespoon chopped fresh chives, plus extra to garnish

For the rostis
4 x 175 g (6 oz) potatoes, unpeeled and grated
1 egg, lightly beaten
calorie controlled cooking spray
salt and freshly ground black pepper

1 Preheat the oven to its lowest setting. Make the rostis. Transfer the grated potatoes to a large bowl. Add the egg and season well.

2 Spray a large non-stick frying pan with the cooking spray and set over a medium heat. Divide the potato mixture into 8, and form into flat patties. Add to the frying pan and cook for 10 minutes, turning once, until golden, crisp and cooked through. You may need to cook the rostis in batches, or you could cook one large rosti. Transfer to a baking sheet in the oven to keep warm.

3 Wipe out the frying pan, and spray again with the cooking spray. Heat over a medium-high heat and add the chicken. Cook for 5–7 minutes until cooked through and starting to brown. Add the mushrooms and tomatoes and cook for a further 3–4 minutes.

4 Remove from the heat, add the quark and fresh herbs, and loosely stir through the chicken mixture, or spoon on top of the chicken to serve, as preferred. Serve the rostis with the chicken mixture and extra herbs to garnish.

Cook's tip If you prefer, use reduced fat crème fraîche instead of the quark, using **ProPoints** values from your weekly allowance.

SWEET POTATO
and Spinach Curry

Put a delicious spicy curry on the table in just half an hour.

Serves up to 4
Takes 30 minutes

calorie controlled cooking spray
1 large onion, chopped finely
500 g (1 lb 2 oz) sweet potatoes,
    peeled and cut into 1 cm (½ inch)
    cubes
1 garlic clove, chopped finely
1 tablespoon Madras curry powder
a pinch of ground cinnamon
400 g can cherry tomatoes
400 g can chick peas, drained
    and rinsed
200 ml (7 fl oz) vegetable stock,
    from a cube
150 g (5½ oz) baby spinach
salt and freshly ground black pepper

To serve
240 g (8½ oz) dried brown basmati
    rice, cooked according to the
    packet instructions
2 tablespoons 0% fat Greek yogurt
2 tablespoons chopped fresh
    coriander

1 Spray a large lidded saucepan with the cooking spray and add the onion and sweet potato. Cook for 5–7 minutes until the onion is softened. Stir in the garlic, curry powder and cinnamon, and cook for a further minute.

2 Add the cherry tomatoes and chick peas along with the vegetable stock. Bring to the boil, cover and simmer for 20 minutes until the sweet potato is tender. Stir in the spinach and cook for a further minute until wilted.

3 Remove the curry from the heat and leave to stand for 1 minute. Season to taste. Serve immediately with brown basmati rice and the yogurt mixed with coriander.

Cook's tip Instead of stock, use reduced fat coconut milk, using *ProPoints* values from your weekly allowance.

SPAGHETTI
Carbonara

A really quick and easy carbonara that's made without any cream.

Serves up to 4
Takes 20 minutes

400 g (14 oz) dried wholewheat
    spaghetti
calorie controlled cooking spray
4 bacon medallions, chopped
2 eggs, lightly beaten
200 g (7 oz) quark
salt and freshly ground black pepper

To garnish
finely chopped fresh chives
basil leaves

1 Bring a large pan of water to the boil. Add the spaghetti, stir well and cook for 12–14 minutes, until al dente, or according to the packet instructions.

2 Meanwhile, spray a small non-stick frying pan with the cooking spray and cook the bacon over a high heat, stirring often, for 4–5 minutes until crisp and browned. Remove from the heat.

3 Mix together the eggs and quark in a large serving bowl. Once the pasta is cooked, drain, reserving about 100 ml (3½ fl oz) of the cooking water. Add the pasta to the bowl with the eggs and quark mixture, along with the cooked bacon. Mix together, adding enough of the cooking water to make a smooth sauce. Season to taste.

4 Serve immediately, garnished with a few chopped chives and basil leaves.

Cook's tips You could preheat the serving bowl by filling it with boiling water, then draining and drying it before you add the eggs and quark.

Add 1–2 tablespoons of grated Parmesan from your weekly *ProPoints* allowance to the eggs and quark mixture.

MOROCCAN TUNA STEAK
with a Roasted Pepper Salsa

Ras el hanout is a North African spice mix. There is no definitive mixture, but it usually contains cardamom, cinnamon, ground chilli, coriander, cumin and turmeric.

Serves up to 4
Takes 30 minutes

4 x 150 g (5½ oz) fresh tuna steaks
4 teaspoons ras el hanout
350 g (12 oz) wholewheat couscous
500 ml (18 fl oz) boiling water
lemon wedges, to serve
chopped fresh coriander, to garnish

For the roasted pepper salsa
1 red pepper, de-seeded and
    quartered lengthways
1 yellow pepper, de-seeded and
    quartered lengthways
calorie controlled cooking spray
200 g (7 oz) cherry tomatoes,
    quartered
1 red onion, finely chopped
1 garlic clove, crushed
juice of 1 lemon
salt and freshly ground black pepper

1 Preheat the grill to high. Pat the tuna steaks dry, and sprinkle each with 1 teaspoon of ras el hanout, rubbing it into both sides.

2 For the salsa, put the peppers, skin side up, on to a baking sheet and spray with the cooking spray. Put them under the grill, as close as you can, and cook for 5 minutes or until the skin is blistered and blackened. Remove from the heat and transfer to a bowl. Cover the bowl with cling film and leave for 5 minutes. Remove the skins as best you can, and finely chop the peppers.

3 Put the peppers, tomatoes, onion, garlic and lemon juice in a serving bowl and mix well. Season to taste and set aside.

4 Meanwhile, put the couscous in another large bowl and add the boiling water. Cover the bowl with a clean tea towel and leave to stand for 6 minutes while you cook the fish.

5 Heat a ridged grill pan over a high heat. Spray the tuna steaks on both sides with the cooking spray and cook for 2–3 minutes on each side, or until done to your taste. Do not overcook – the fish should still be a little pink in the middle.

6 Serve the fish immediately with the couscous, the roasted pepper salsa and lemon wedges, and sprinkled with fresh coriander.

PRAWN, MUSHROOM
and Chick Pea Curry

This filling curry dish is great served with a fresh tomato sambal.

Serves 4
Takes 25 minutes

❄ *Freeze before adding the prawns*

calorie controlled cooking spray
1 onion, chopped finely
1 garlic clove, crushed
1 teaspoon grated fresh root ginger
100 g (3½ oz) button mushrooms,
  halved
1 tablespoon curry powder
1 teaspoon ground coriander
1 tomato, chopped
100 ml (3½ fl oz) vegetable or fish
  stock, from a cube
400 g can chick peas, drained and
  rinsed
300 g (10½ oz) cooked prawns
4 tablespoons 0% fat Greek yogurt
3 tablespoons chopped fresh
  coriander, plus a few sprigs to
  garnish
salt and freshly ground black pepper

To serve
240 g (8½ oz) dried brown basmati
  rice, cooked according to the
  packet instructions

1 Spray a medium saucepan with the cooking spray and heat over a medium heat. Add the onion and cook for 3–4 minutes until softened, then add the garlic and ginger. Cook briefly before adding the mushrooms. Cook for a further 5 minutes, then add the curry powder and ground coriander. Stir briefly and add the tomato, vegetable or fish stock and chick peas. It may seem like there isn't enough liquid, but don't be tempted to add more at this stage. Stir well and bring to the boil.

2 Cook the curry, uncovered, for 10 minutes until thickened and reduced. Add the prawns and remove from the heat. Leave to stand for 5 minutes, then stir in the yogurt and coriander. Season to taste and serve with brown basmati rice, garnished with coriander sprigs.

Cook's tips Serve with a fresh tomato sambal: chopped tomatoes mixed with finely chopped green chilli, finely chopped spring onions and chopped fresh coriander.

For this recipe, you could grate the tomato instead of chopping it as this helps it break down much quicker.

WARM BEETROOT
and Smoked Trout Salad

This quick salad is great for a summer evening meal in the garden.

Serves up to 4
Takes 20 minutes

500 g (1 lb 2 oz) new potatoes, sliced thickly
100 g bag mixed salad leaves
125 g (4½ oz) smoked trout fillets, flaked
250 g (9 oz) cooked beetroot, cut into wedges
2 celery sticks, sliced finely
chopped fresh dill, to garnish

For the dressing
4 tablespoons virtually fat-free fromage frais
4 radishes, grated finely, or 2 teaspoons grated fresh horseradish
juice of ½ lemon
1 tablespoon chopped fresh dill
4 teaspoons extra virgin olive oil
salt and freshly ground black pepper

1 Cover the potatoes with cold water, bring to the boil and cook for 6–8 minutes or until just tender.

2 For the dressing, whisk together the fromage frais, radishes or horseradish, lemon juice to taste, dill and olive oil. Season to taste.

3 Drain the potatoes and cool slightly. Mix with the dressing.

4 Serve the salad leaves, trout, beetroot and celery topped with the warm dressed potatoes, garnished with some chopped fresh dill.

Cook's tips For extra crunch, add some toasted walnuts using **ProPoints** values from your weekly allowance.

If you prefer horseradish and can't find fresh, add 2 teaspoons of grated horseradish from a jar, using **ProPoints** values from your weekly allowance.

GAMMON STEAK
with Peaches and Roast Potato Chunks

This is a great weekday dish.

Serves up to 4
Takes 35 minutes

4 x 175 g (6 oz) potatoes, cut into
  small chunks
calorie controlled cooking spray
3 ripe peaches or nectarines
2 tablespoons grainy mustard
4 x 175 g (6 oz) gammon steaks,
  visible fat removed
salt and freshly ground black pepper

To serve
steamed green vegetables

1 Preheat the oven to Gas Mark 6/200°C/fan oven 180°C. Spread the potatoes on a non-stick baking tray in a single layer and spray with the cooking spray. Season well. Transfer to an upper shelf in the oven and cook for 15 minutes.

2 Meanwhile, peel one of the peaches – the skin should peel off easily as they are ripe – and chop roughly. Put the peach in a small saucepan with 1 tablespoon of water. Bring to the boil then reduce the heat and simmer for 5 minutes until the peach starts to break down. Remove from the heat and mash roughly with a fork. Stir in the mustard and some black pepper. Halve and stone the remaining 2 peaches, then cut into thick wedges.

3 Lay the gammon steaks on a baking sheet and divide the peach and mustard glaze between them. Add the peach wedges to the baking sheet. Spray the peaches and gammon with cooking spray.

4 Take the potatoes out, turn them and return to the oven. Put the gammon and peaches on the shelf below the potatoes and cook them for 10 minutes. Take the potatoes out after 5 minutes – they should be golden and crispy.

5 If necessary, flash the gammon steaks and peach wedges under a hot grill until golden. Serve immediately with the potatoes and green vegetables.

Cook's tip Keep a careful eye on the gammon steaks – the peach and mustard glaze has a tendency to catch.

STEAK
and Mushroom Stroganoff

Creamy, comforting and very speedy to make – an ideal midweek supper.

Serves up to 4
Takes 20 minutes

calorie controlled cooking spray
1 onion, sliced thinly
1 green pepper, de-seeded and
    sliced thinly
200 g (7 oz) button mushrooms,
    sliced thinly
1 garlic clove, chopped
1 teaspoon paprika
2 tablespoons red wine vinegar
150 ml (5 fl oz) beef stock,
    from a cube
350 g (12 oz) lean sirloin steak,
    trimmed of visible fat and
    sliced thinly
150 g (5½ oz) virtually fat-free
    fromage frais
1 tablespoon chopped fresh parsley
salt and freshly ground black pepper

To serve
240 g (8½ oz) dried wholewheat
    tagliatelle, cooked according to
    the packet instructions

1 Spray a large frying pan with the cooking spray and set over a medium heat. Add the onion, green pepper and mushrooms and cook for 5–7 minutes, until the vegetables are softened. Add the garlic and stir briefly.

2 Stir in the paprika to mix. Add the vinegar and allow to bubble and reduce until almost evaporated, then add the beef stock. Bring to the boil and simmer for a minute or two until slightly thickened.

3 Add the steak, stir well, and cook for 2–3 minutes until the beef is cooked through (or a little less if you like your beef rare). Remove from the heat and stir through the fromage frais and parsley. Season to taste. Serve with wholewheat tagliatelle.

Cook's tip Use low fat crème fraîche instead of fromage frais, using *ProPoints* values from your weekly allowance.

STEAK AND CHUNKY CHIPS
with Herbed Hollandaise

You could also use lean sirloin steak if you prefer; reduce the
cooking times accordingly, as sirloin tends to be thinner.

Serves up to 4
Takes 25 minutes

4 x 250 g (9 oz) potatoes, cut into
   chunky chips
1 teaspoon dried mixed herbs
calorie controlled cooking spray
4 x 150 g (5½ oz) fillet steaks, visible
   fat removed
1 garlic clove
4 sprigs of cherry tomatoes on
   the vine
salt and freshly ground black pepper
cooked asparagus spears, to serve

For the herbed hollandaise
2 eggs
1 teaspoon Dijon mustard
1 tablespoon white wine vinegar
2 tablespoons finely chopped fresh
   herbs, such as basil, tarragon,
   thyme, parsley, chives

1 Preheat the oven to Gas Mark 7/220°C/fan oven 200°C. Spread
the chips on a large baking sheet, sprinkle with the mixed herbs
and season. Spray with the cooking spray and toss to mix. Make
sure the chips are in a single layer before transferring them to the
top of the oven. Cook for 15 minutes, then turn and cook for a
further 5–10 minutes until golden and crisp.

2 To make the hollandaise, put the eggs, mustard and vinegar in
a heatproof bowl with 6 tablespoons of water. Set the bowl over a
pan of simmering water so that the bowl doesn't touch the water.
Whisk constantly until the sauce thickens and becomes light and
foamy – about 4–5 minutes. Stir in the chopped herbs and season
to taste. Set aside while you cook the steaks.

3 Preheat a ridged grill pan over a high heat. Rub the fillet steaks
on both sides with the garlic clove and season well. Put the steaks
carefully on the grill pan and cook to taste – see Cook's tip (below).
Remove the steaks to a plate to rest while the chips finish cooking.
While the steaks are resting, put the tomatoes on the grill pan.

4 Serve the chips and steaks with the sauce spooned over,
alongside the asparagus and cherry tomatoes.

Cook's tip To time your steak to perfection, follow these
guidelines: 2–3 minutes on each side for rare, 3–4 each side for
medium rare, 4–5 each side for medium to medium well, and
5–6 minutes each side for well done.

GREEK PORK PATTIES
with Radish Tzatziki

These delicious patties would also be perfect served
as part of a larger meze platter.

Serves up to 4
Takes 20 minutes

500 g (1 lb 2 oz) extra lean pork
   mince
1 red onion, grated
2 teaspoons dried oregano
zest of 1 lemon
1 garlic clove, crushed
25 g (1 oz) breadcrumbs, made from
   calorie controlled brown bread
calorie controlled cooking spray
4 Weight Watchers pitta breads
salt and freshly ground black pepper

For the radish tzatziki
200 g (7 oz) 0% fat Greek yogurt
8 radishes, grated coarsely or
   chopped
1 garlic clove, crushed

For the tomato salad
4 tomatoes, cut into chunks
1 small red onion, sliced finely
2 teaspoons red wine vinegar
4 teaspoons extra virgin olive oil

To serve
a handful of watercress

1 Preheat the grill to high. Put the pork mince in a large bowl and add the onion, oregano, lemon zest, garlic and breadcrumbs. Season well and mix everything together. Divide the mixture into 8 and shape into small, flat patties.

2 Transfer the patties to a baking sheet and spray with the cooking spray. Grill for 5–6 minutes on each side until golden and cooked through.

3 Meanwhile, make the tzatziki. Mix together the yogurt, radishes and garlic, and season.

4 Make the tomato salad by mixing together the tomatoes, onion, vinegar and olive oil, and season.

5 When the patties are cooked, transfer them to a plate. Toast the pitta breads under the grill and serve immediately with the pork patties, tzatziki, tomato salad and some watercress.

Cook's tip Add some feta or low fat goat's cheese using **ProPoints** values from your weekly allowance.

BACON AND WHITE BEAN
Casserole

A deliciously warming stew that's ready in no time.

Serves up to 4
Takes 30 minutes

calorie controlled cooking spray
6 bacon medallions, sliced finely
1 onion, chopped finely
1 carrot, chopped finely
1 celery stick, chopped finely
1 garlic clove, chopped finely
1 tablespoon chopped fresh thyme
2 tomatoes, chopped roughly
2 x 400 g cans haricot beans, drained
    and rinsed
400–500 ml (14–18 fl oz) chicken or
    vegetable stock, from a cube
zest of 1 lemon
2 tablespoons chopped fresh parsley,
    plus extra to garnish
salt and freshly ground black pepper

1 Heat a large lidded non-stick saucepan over a high heat and spray with the cooking spray. Add the bacon and reduce the heat to medium. Cook, stirring often, until golden and crispy – about 5 minutes. Remove about half the bacon and set aside to drain on some kitchen paper, to use as garnish.

2 Add the onion, carrot and celery to the pan, spraying again with cooking spray if necessary. Cook for 7–8 minutes until softened, adding a splash of water to the pan to prevent the vegetables sticking or burning. When they are soft, add the garlic, thyme and tomatoes and stir together for a minute.

3 Add the beans and 400 ml (14 fl oz) of the stock. Bring to the boil, cover and simmer for 15 minutes. Remove about a quarter of the stew and purée it before returning it to the pan, along with the lemon zest and parsley. Season to taste. Add enough of the remaining stock to make a thick stew texture.

4 Serve immediately, garnished with the reserved bacon and sprinkled with a little chopped parsley.

Cook's tip Serve with a chunk of French bread using ***ProPoints*** values from your weekly allowance.

PORK ESCALOPES
with Caponata Salad

This marinade also works well with lean loin steaks.

Serves up to 4
Takes 30 minutes

4 x 150 g (5½ oz) pork escalopes,
  sliced thinly

For the marinade
zest and juice of 1 lemon
2 teaspoons dried mint
1 teaspoon dried oregano
1 garlic clove, crushed
2 tablespoons red wine vinegar

For the caponata salad
225 g (8 oz) bulgur wheat
4 large tomatoes, chopped
2 teaspoons capers in vinegar,
  drained
2 spring onions, chopped finely
juice of 1 lemon
4 tablespoons chopped fresh parsley
1 small aubergine, sliced thinly
calorie controlled cooking spray
salt and freshly ground black pepper

To serve
Little Gem lettuce leaves

1 Make the marinade. Mix together the lemon zest and juice, mint, oregano, garlic and vinegar. Put the escalopes in a non-reactive dish and pour over the marinade. Leave to marinate briefly while you make the caponata salad.

2 Put the bulgur wheat in a large saucepan and cover with water. Bring to the boil and simmer for 2 minutes. Remove from the heat and leave to stand for a further 5 minutes, then drain well in a sieve. Run cold water over the bulgur wheat to cool it quickly. Drain well and transfer to a serving bowl. Add the tomatoes, capers, spring onions, lemon juice and parsley. Season well and mix.

3 Preheat a ridged grill pan over a high heat. Spray the aubergine slices with the cooking spray. Add them to the grill pan and cook for 1–2 minutes on each side until golden and cooked through. As they cook, add them to the bulgur wheat mixture.

4 Cook the pork escalopes in the grill pan for 2–3 minutes on each side or until just cooked through. Serve with the caponata salad and some lettuce leaves.

Cook's tip Add some feta cheese to the salad using **ProPoints** values from your weekly allowance.

INDEX

V denotes a vegetarian recipe

ProPoints values index

Recipe	Page	Serves	ProPoints value per serving
Bacon and white bean casserole	90	4	3
Blackened fish with fiery mango salsa (pollock)	42	4	3
Hearty spiced mixed bean soup	14	4	3
Spanish eggs with potatoes and peppers	20	4	4
Spicy beans on toast	24	4	4
Mini chicken, spinach and cottage cheese frittatas	12	4	5
Warm beetroot and smoked trout salad	80	4	5
Butter bean toast topper	18	2	6
Chicken and roasted squash salad	36	4	6
Home-made chip-shop chips with curry sauce	22	4	6
Blackened fish with fiery mango salsa (salmon)	42	4	7
Puy lentils with roasted vegetables and cumin	64	4	7
All-in-one roast chicken with garlic sauce	38	4	8
Cheesy potato topper	16	4	8
Creamy chicken and mushroom rostis	70	4	8
Crispy potato skins	28	4	8
Classic burger with a twist	56	4	9
Jerk fish with rice and peas	48	4	9
Steak and mushroom stroganoff	84	4	9
Chinese-style white fish	26	4	10
Eggs Benedict	30	4	10
Gammon steak with peaches and roast potato chunks	82	4	10
Greek pork patties with radish tzatziki	88	4	10
Pan-fried chicken and asparagus (with penne)	68	4	10
Pork escalopes with caponata salad	92	4	10
Pork and apple hotpot	50	4	11
Prawn, mushroom and chick pea curry (with rice)	78	4	11
Slow-cooked beef meatball stew (with spaghetti)	60	4	11
Turkey club sandwich	10	1	11
Warm spiced quinoa salad	62	4	11
Chicken stew and rice	40	4	12
Sea bass with fennel, potatoes and lemon	44	4	12
Spaghetti carbonara	74	4	12
Steak and chunky chips with herbed hollandaise	86	4	12
Sweet potato and spinach curry (with rice)	72	4	12
Yellow split pea and ham soup	32	4	12
Braising steaks with onions and mushrooms (with baked potato)	58	4	13
Quick chilli con carne (with rice)	52	4	13
Roasted salmon fillet with bacon, peas, potatoes and mint	46	4	13
Jerk fish with rice and peas (salmon)	48	4	14
Moroccan tuna steak with a roasted pepper salsa	76	4	14
Souvlaki pork with kisir	54	4	14